Introduction

The traditional art of paper folding has a long time it was an integral part of religious ceremonies, and in Japan the folded crane is still considered a symbol of good luck. Your creations will look amazing in the various kawaii patterns. This book will help you to fold your own magnificent animals and other figures quickly and easily.

On the following pages, you will find a selection of folding instructions that you can use to make some impressive origami pieces. Thanks to the 333 cute kawaii pattern papers, there are endless combinations and folding possibilities.

Happy folding!

The Basics

BASIC SHAPE: KITE

1. To make a diagonal fold, position the paper so that one corner is facing you. Take the corner and fold it over to meet the opposite corner. Make a crease and then unfold the sheet.

2. Fold the outer edges of the paper inward to line up with the diagonal crease you have just made.

ZIGZAG FOLD

1. Fold the paper inward on the first marked line and outward on the second.

2. Fold inward again on the second fold and then fold outward on the first fold.

Finished!

The kite is the basic shape for the **rabbit** and **chicken**.

Finished!

The zigzag fold is used when making the **turtle**, **rabbit**, and **chicken**.

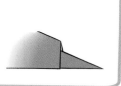

INSIDE REVERSE FOLD

1. Fold the tip inward and then unfold.

2. Gently pull the sides outward and fold the point down (between the sides).

OUTSIDE REVERSE FOLD

1. Fold the tip inward and then unfold.

2. Gently pull the sides outward and down, and fold the point over them (over the sides).

 Finished!

The inside reverse fold is used to form the head of bird figures, such as the **dove** and **crane**.

Finished!

The outside reverse fold is another way of making bird heads. This fold makes the head a little sturdier and is used for the **penguin** and **chicken**.

Heart

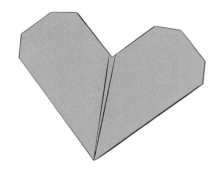

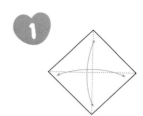

Make two diagonal folds by placing the opposite corners on top of each other, and then open out the sheet.

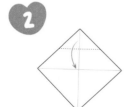

Fold the top corner down to meet the centerline.

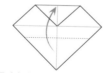

Fold the bottom corner right up to the top edge.

Fold the bottom left and right edges into the center and turn the whole thing over.

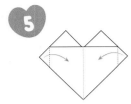

Fold the left and right corners toward the center.

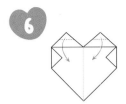

Fold the top two corners down.

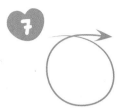

Turn the shape over.

 Finished!

The heart is ready. You may want to write a greeting on it or give it to someone as a gift. You could open up the two sides of the heart and write a loving message inside.

Fish

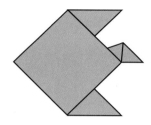

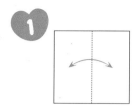

1 Place the sheet with the patterned side facing down and make a vertical fold down the center. Open out the sheet.

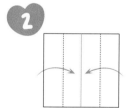

2 Fold the left and right edges inward to meet the central crease.

3 Fold the bottom edge up to meet the top edge and open out the sheet again.

4 Fold the top and bottom edges to meet the horizontal crease you have just made.

Take the small square you now have and fold along the two diagonals.

Fold one side of the square up and pull the left and right center points of the sheet up and out to the sides to create two triangles.

Turn the shape 180°; then fold the other edge upward and proceed as in Step 6.

Now turn the shape 90°. Open out the top right triangle and fold it into a small square toward the center.

Fold the two left triangles to the left along the central line.

To make the fin, fold the lower of the two triangles down and turn over the shape.

Finished!

Pinwheel

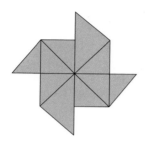

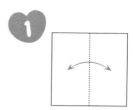

1

Place the sheet with the patterned side facing down and make a vertical fold down the center. Open out the sheet.

2

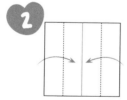

Fold the left and right edges inward to meet the central crease.

3

Fold the bottom edge up to meet the top edge and open out the sheet again.

4

Fold the top and bottom edges to meet the horizontal crease you have just made.

Take the small square you now have and fold along the two diagonals.

Fold one side of the square up and pull the top layer of the sheet to the sides to create two triangles.

Turn the shape 180°; then fold the other edge upward and proceed as in Step 6.

Fold the top right corner up and the bottom left corner down, as shown.

Finished!

To make the pinwheel turn, you can take a paper fastener and pierce it through the center to secure the windmill to a wooden stick.

Cricket

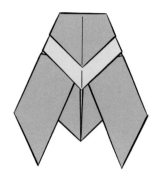

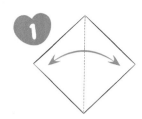

1 Make a diagonal fold by placing two opposite corners together and opening them.

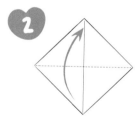

2 Make a second diagonal fold with the other two corners, but do not open out the sheet when you are done.

3 Take the two corners of the long edge and fold them to the tip of the triangle.

4 Now fold the same corners down and slightly outwards.

Now the tip of the top layer is folded down.

Fold the back layer down, slightly above the top layer.

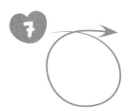

Turn the figure over.

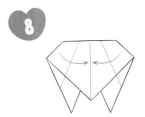

Fold the left and right sides towards the middle.

Fold and unfold the outer corners.

Turn the figure over again.

Finished!

Crane

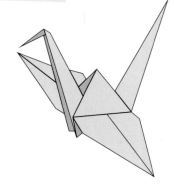

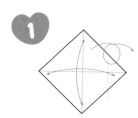

1 Make two diagonal folds, then open out the sheet and turn it over.

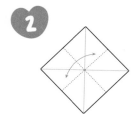

2 Fold the two parallel diagonals and open out the sheet again.

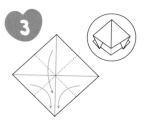

3 Place a finger on the center of the sheet so that the sides start to fold up. Now push the prefolded shape together.

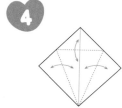

4 Position the folded shape in front of you so that the open tip is facing you. Fold the left and right edges in toward the central crease, then fold the top corner down.

5

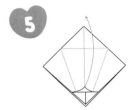

Fold the bottom corner upward and the outer edges will automatically move to the center.

6

Turn the shape over and fold the bottom corner up as in the previous step.

7

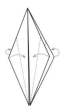

Fold the left and right corners toward the center. Turn the shape over again and repeat the process on the other side.

8

Use two inside reverse folds to make the crane's tail and neck.

9

Now make the head using one inside reverse fold, and fold the wings out to the sides.

✔ Finished!

In Japan, cranes are the symbol of a happy life. Legend also says that if you make 1,000 origami cranes, you can make a wish. So go ahead—your crane will be really glad to have some company.

Turtle

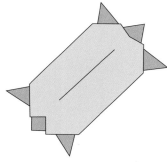

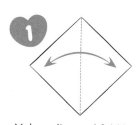

1

Make a diagonal fold by placing two opposite corners on top of each other, then open out the sheet again.

2

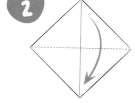

Make a second diagonal fold with the other two opposite corners, but do not open out the sheet after.

3

Take the two corners of the long edge and fold them down to the tip of the triangle.

4

Now fold the same two corners upward.

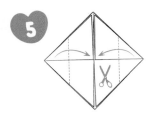

5 Cut a slit in the top layer of the sheet from the bottom corner to the center, and fold the right and left corners in toward the center.

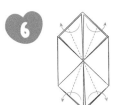

6 Fold the top and bottom tips outward.

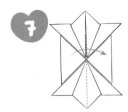

7 Fold the whole shape once vertically in the center.

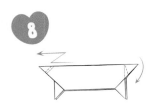

8 On one side, make a zigzag fold for the tail then make another one on the other side for the head, according to the fold lines shown.

9 Unfold the shape.

✔ Finished!

You've just made your first origami turtle! It's a real eye-catcher with its colorful shell—you can certainly expect to receive lots of compliments.

Rabbit

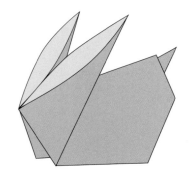

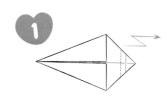

1

Start by making a kite shape and then make a zigzag fold at the top point.

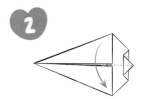

2

Now fold the whole shape horizontally along the center.

3

Fold the tip outward and upward.

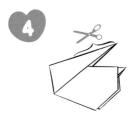

4

Cut the tip about two-thirds of the way along the fold and open it to form the rabbit's ears.

Finished!

Penguin

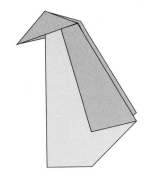

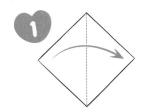

1 Make a diagonal fold by placing two opposite corners on top of each other.

2 Take the outer corners of the triangle and fold them inward on both sides, then open out the triangle.

3 Fold the bottom corner up, then fold the whole shape along the central crease.

4 Make an outside reverse fold for the head.

Finished!

Dove

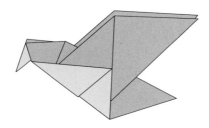

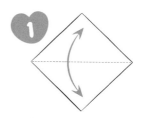

1 Make a diagonal fold by placing two opposite corners on top of each other and then open out the sheet.

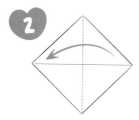

2 Make a second diagonal fold with the other two corners, but do not open out the sheet when you are done.

3 Take the tip of the triangle and fold about two-thirds of it to the right so that it slightly overlaps the long edge.

4 Open the triangle up by taking the top layer and folding about two-thirds of it to the left.

Fold the top half of the shape down so that the top corner lines up with the bottom corner.

Now fold the "wings" up.

Make the head using an inside reverse fold.

 Finished!

Now your dove is ready to take flight. With its beautiful pattern, it makes a great wedding gift and lives up to its meaning as a bringer of peace!

Chicken

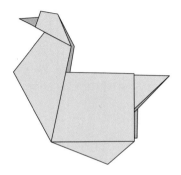

Start with a kite shape.

Make a zigzag fold at the top.

Fold the figure in half.

Turn the figure over.

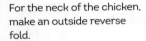

For the neck of the chicken, make an outside reverse fold.

Make another outside reverse fold for the head. Then fold up the bottom right corner to form the wing tips and repeat on the back.

For the beak, make a zigzag fold and the chicken is ready!

Finished!

This origami chicken is particularly beautiful in the Easter basket. Its patterned plumage goes wonderfully with colorful Easter eggs.

Snake

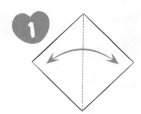

1 Make a diagonal fold by placing two opposite corners on top of each other, then open out the sheet.

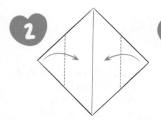

2 Fold the outer corners in toward the center.

3 Fold the outside edges in again toward the center.

4 Fold the sides in once more.

Fold the bottom corner up toward the center.

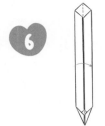

Fold the shape in half vertically.

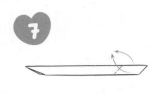

Fold the front section upward to make an outside reverse fold for the neck.

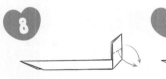

Make another outside reverse fold for the head.

Make alternating inward and outward folds for the snake's body.

Finished!

Butterfly

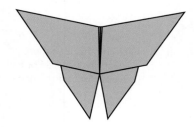

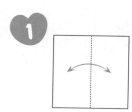

1

Place the sheet with the patterned side facing down and make a vertical fold in the center. Open out the sheet.

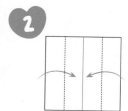

2

Fold the left and right edges in toward the center.

3

Fold the bottom edge up to meet the top edge and open out the sheet again.

4

Fold the top and bottom edges to meet the horizontal crease you have just made.

Take the small square you now have and fold along the two diagonals.

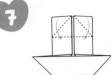

Fold one side of the square up and pull the left and right center points of the sheet up and out to the sides to create two triangles.

Turn the shape 180°; then fold the other edge upward and proceed as in Step 6.

Fold down the left and right corners.

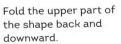

Fold the upper part of the shape back and downward.

Fold the two corners into the center. Fold the whole thing once in the center and turn it over.

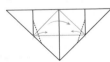

Finished!

333 Origami Sheets Kawaii Designs

First published in the United States in 2024 by C&T Publishing, Inc., P.O. Box 1456, Lafayette, CA 94549

EMF © Edition Michael Fischer GmbH, 2023

www.emf-verlag.de

This edition of "333 ORIGAMI – KAWAII" first published in Germany by Edition Michael Fischer GmbH in 2023 is published by arrangement with Silke Bruenink Agency, Munich, Germany.

PUBLISHER: Amy Barrett-Daffin

CREATIVE DIRECTOR: Gailen Runge

SENIOR ACQUISITIONS EDITOR: Roxane Cerda

PRODUCT MANAGER: Betsy La Honta

ENGLISH-LANGUAGE COVER DESIGNER: April Mostek

ENGLISH TRANSLATION: Krista Hold and Gailen Runge

PRODUCTION COORDINATOR: Zinnia Heinzmann

Graphics instructions section EMF, except: © tofang/Shutterstock (pinwheel, fish, crane, heart, butterfly)

Images from Shutterstock:

Pattern cover: © Alef-Beth, © ma_nud_sen, © Palomita

Pattern yellow: 2x © tannikart, 2x © Gabriyel Onat, © ma_nud_sen, © Aleandro, © Katsiaryna Pleshakova, © Kotova Liudmila

Pattern pink: © Alef-Beth, © Samoilova Natalya, 3x © ma_nud_sen, © tannikart, © Viaire, © AliceFoster

Pattern blue: © Snezhana Togoi, © palasha, © Svetlana Tokarenko, © AllNikArt, © Povitrulya, © Linda Ayu Pertiwi, © Professor Purr, © Kristina Rudkevica

Pattern green: © yuda chen, © mhatzapa, © YetiCub, © ma_nud_sen, © svtdesign, © Gabriyel Onat, © Pani Monica, © PashkovaTetiana

Pattern grey/brown: © Bijoy Designs, © Torico, © ma_nud_sen, © Aleandro, © Palomita, © CraftCloud, © PraePaints, © svtdesign

Printed in China

10 9 8 7 6 5 4 3 2 1

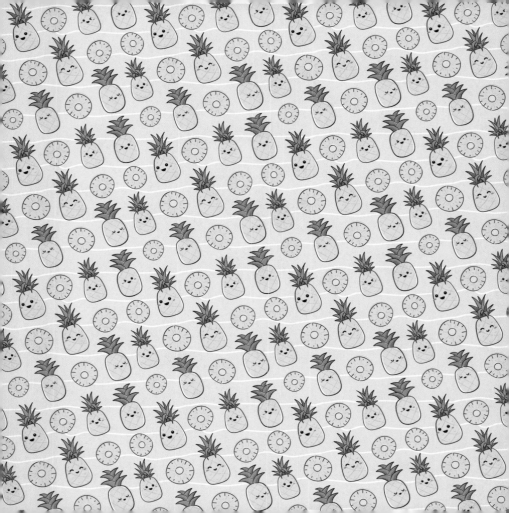

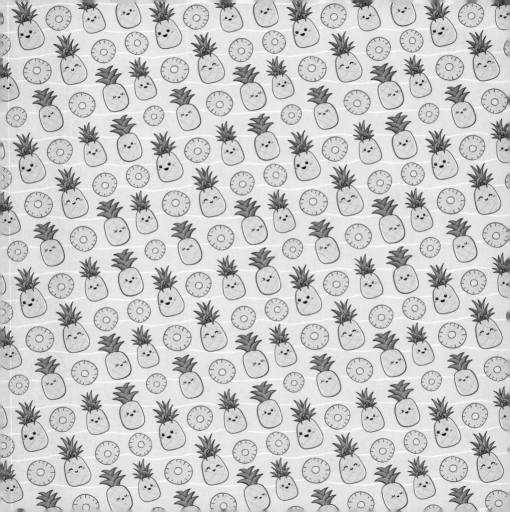

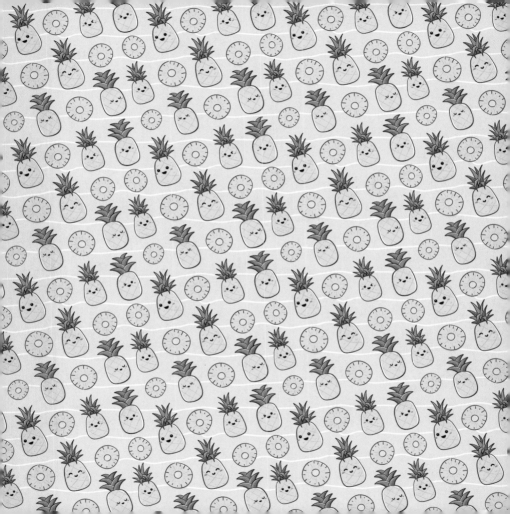

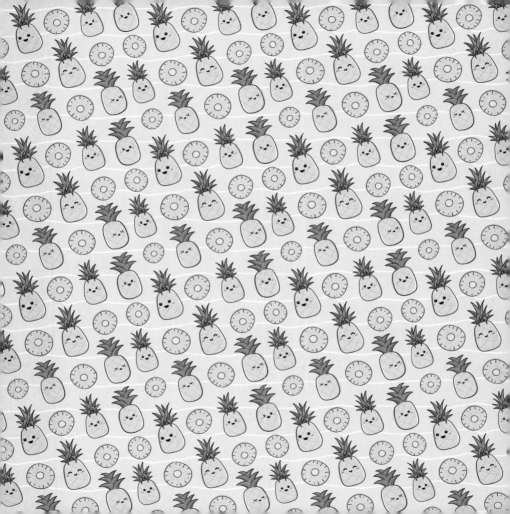

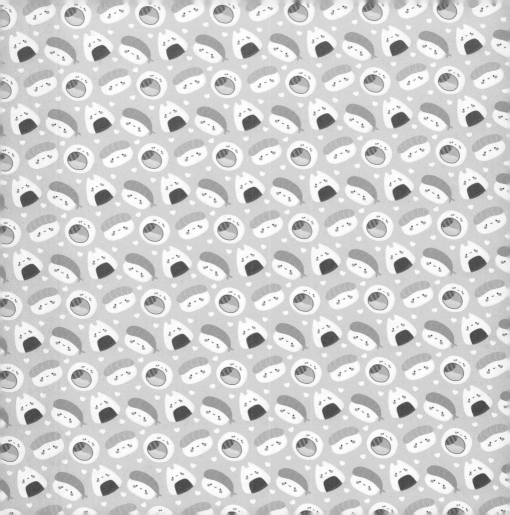

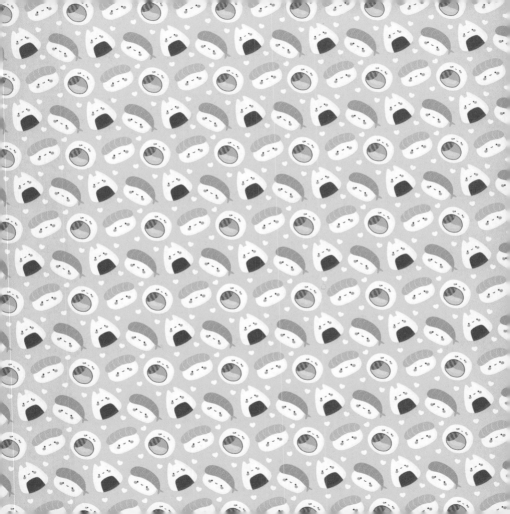

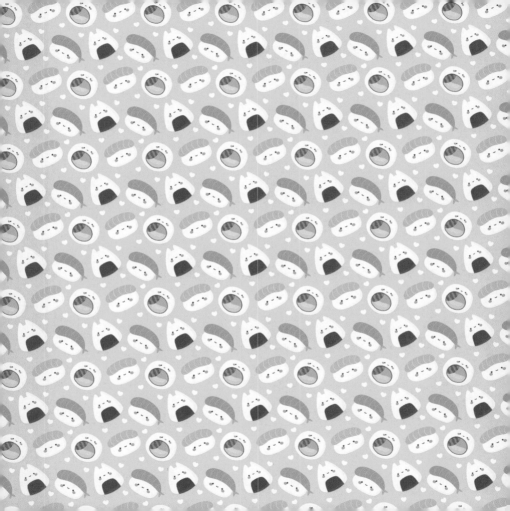

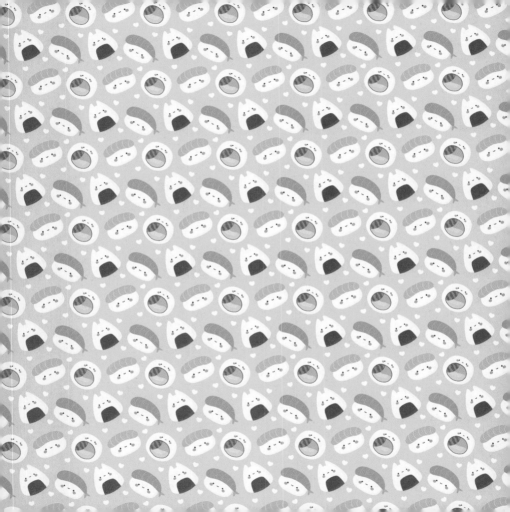

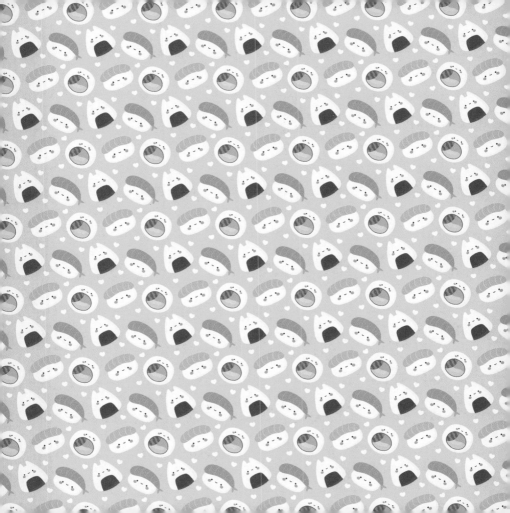

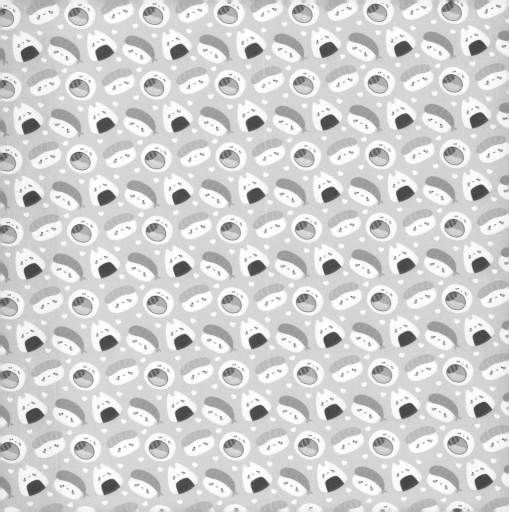

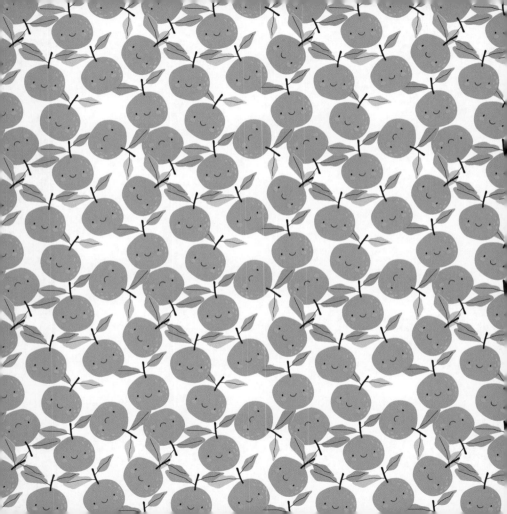

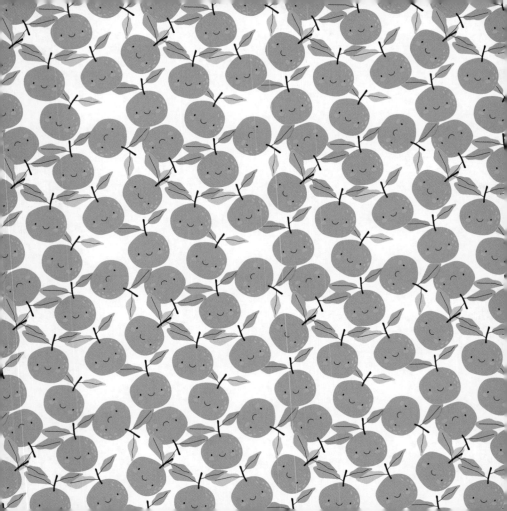

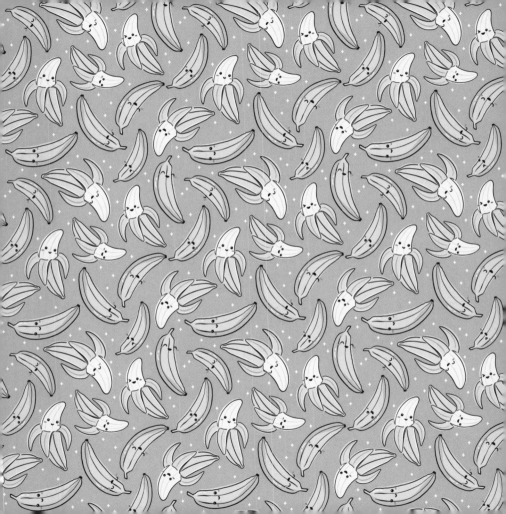

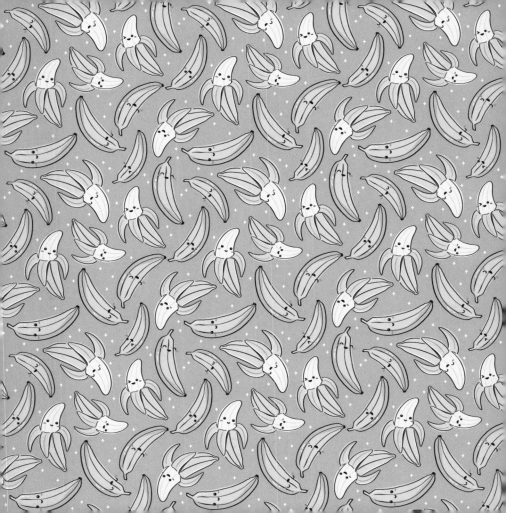

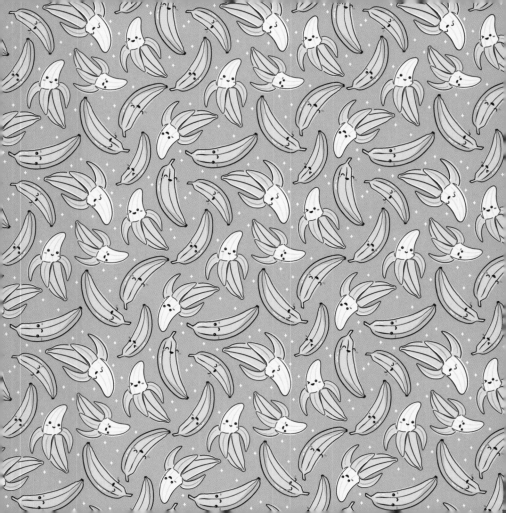

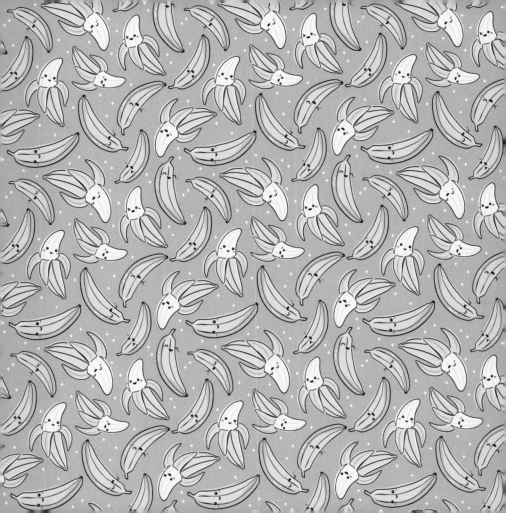

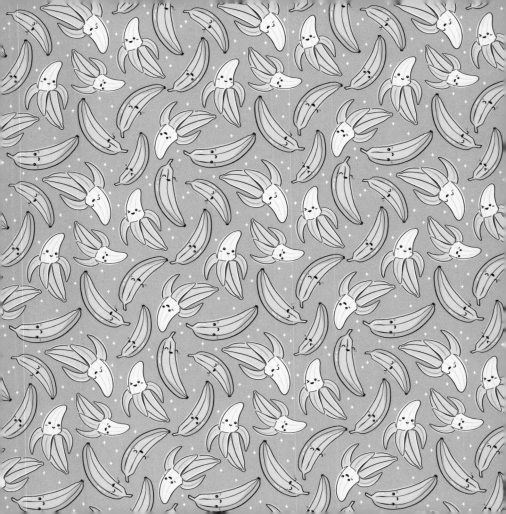

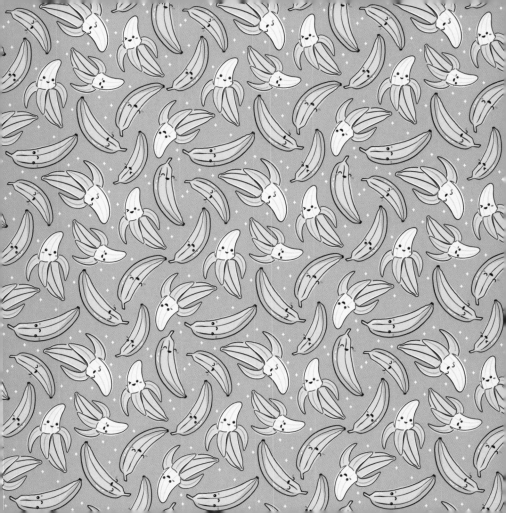

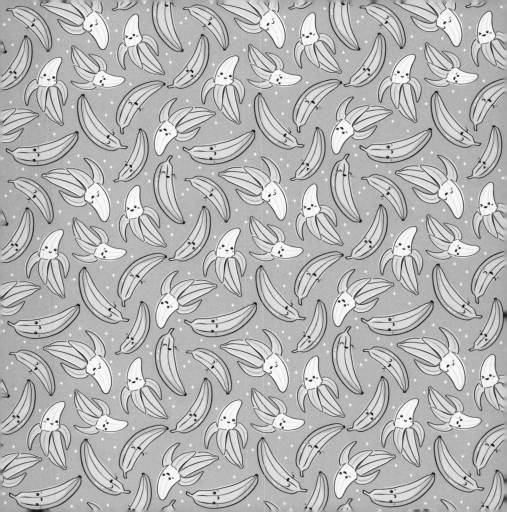

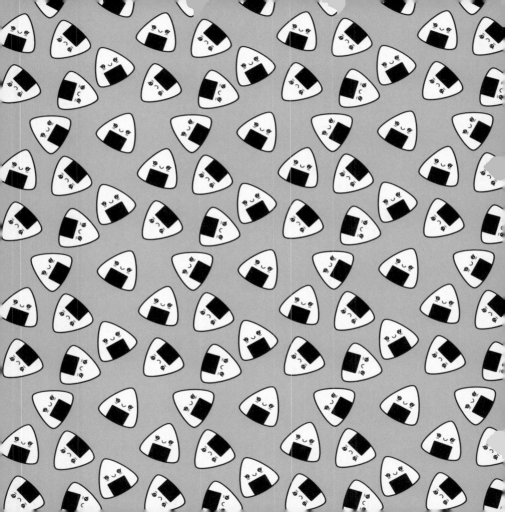

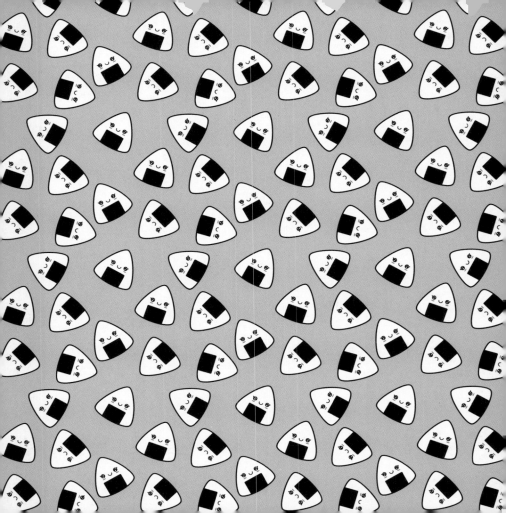

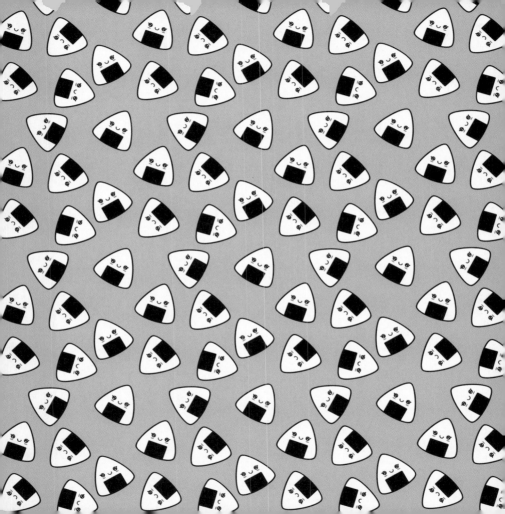

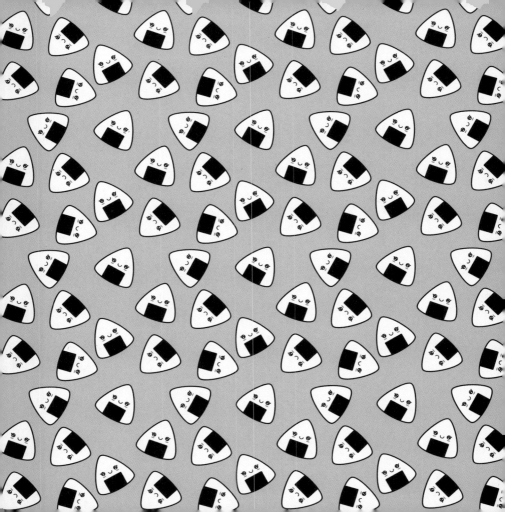

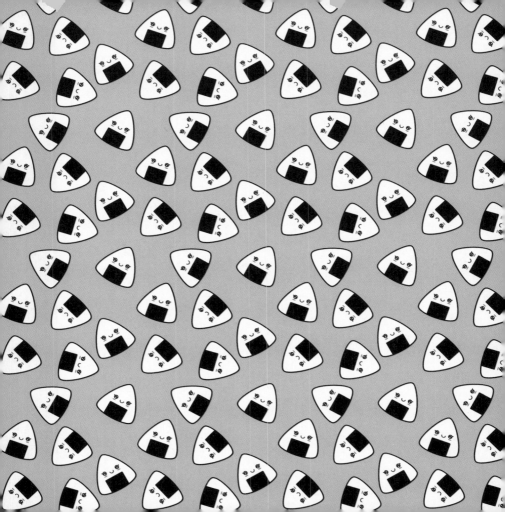

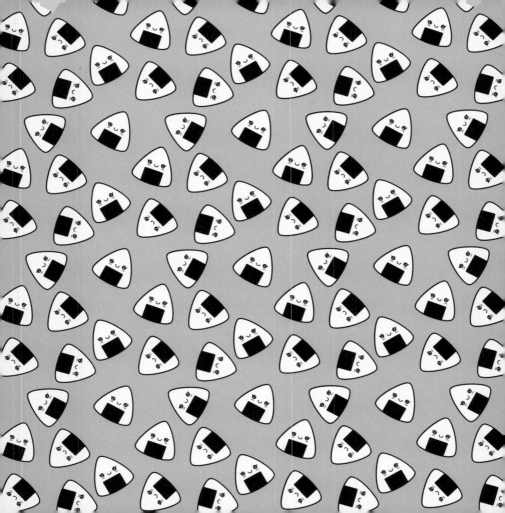

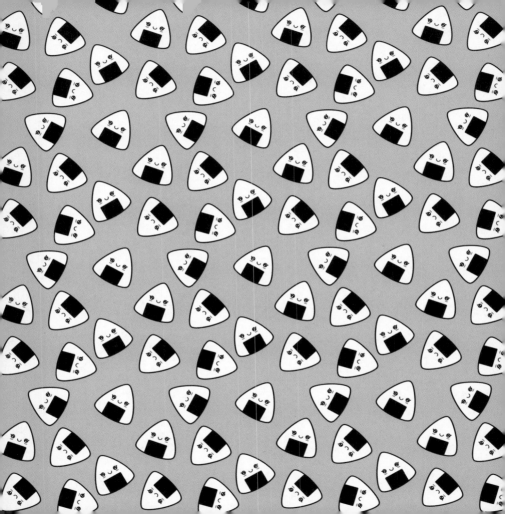

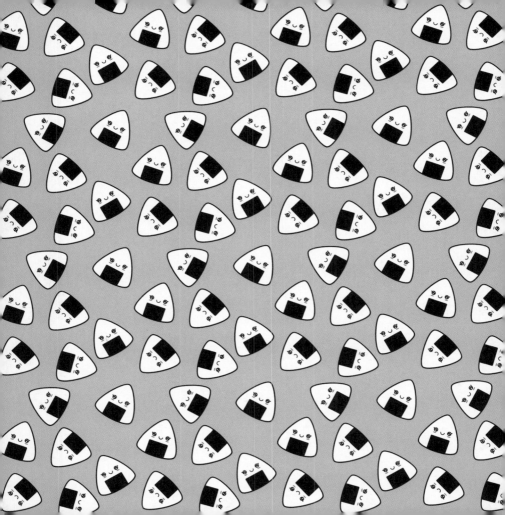

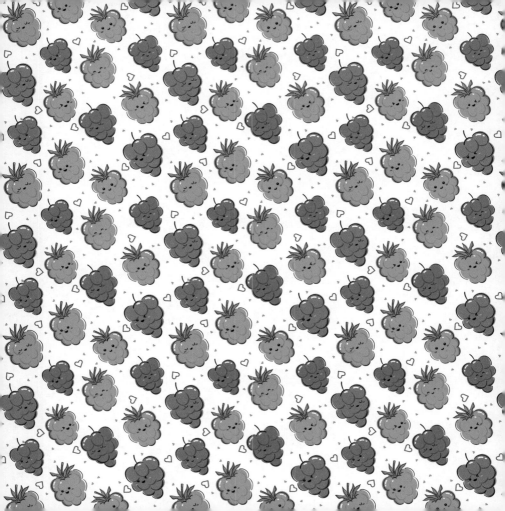

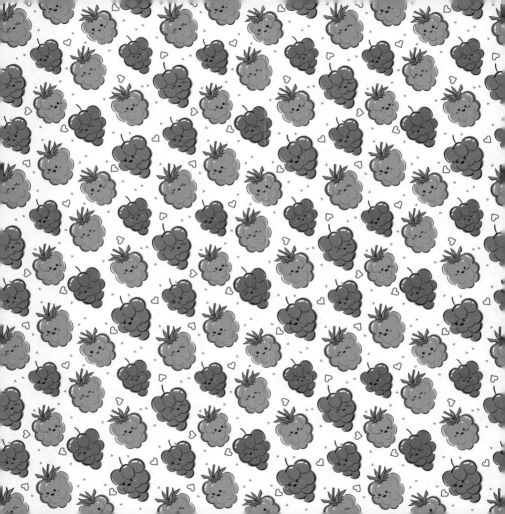

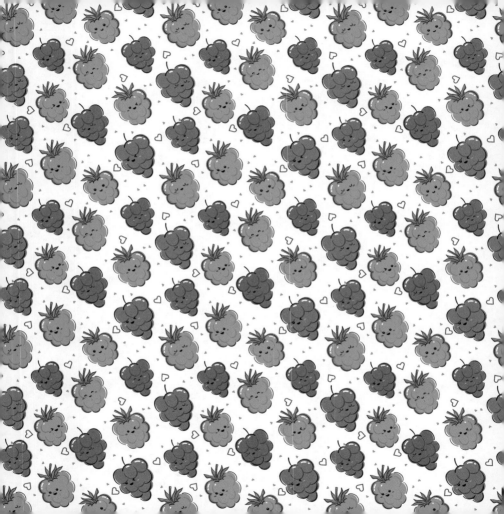

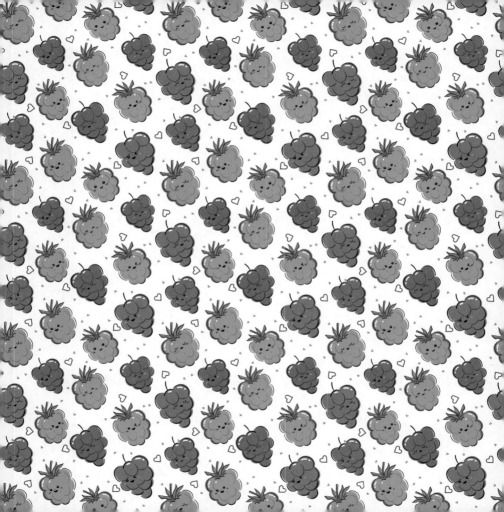

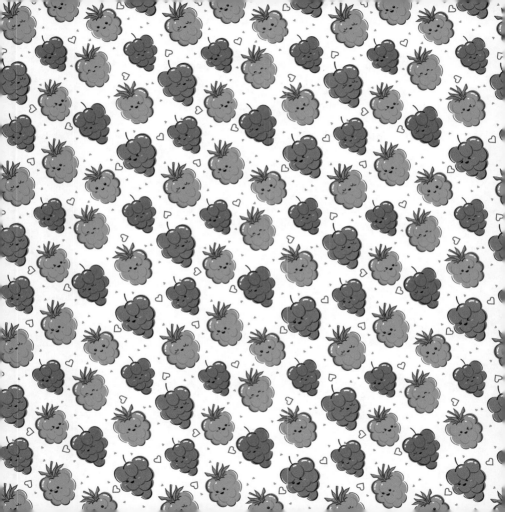

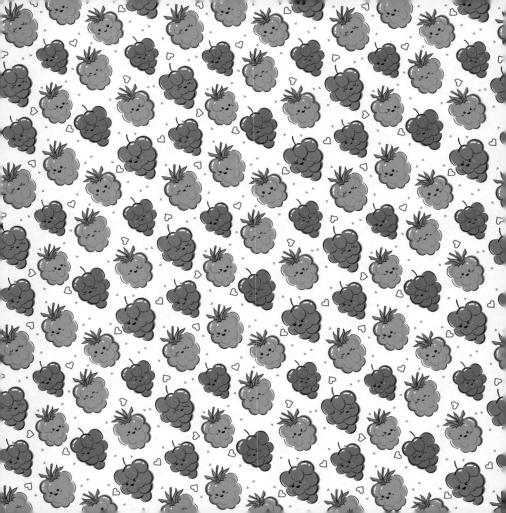

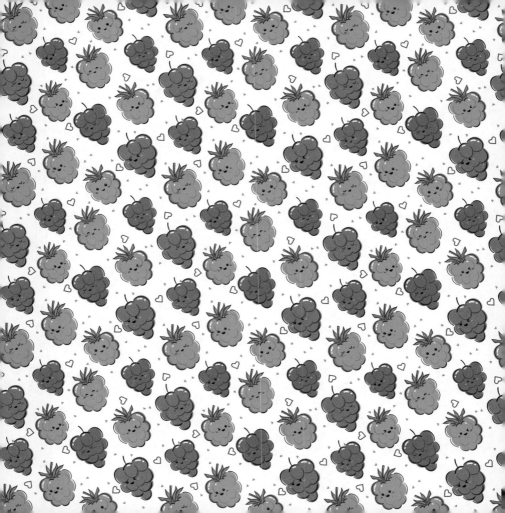

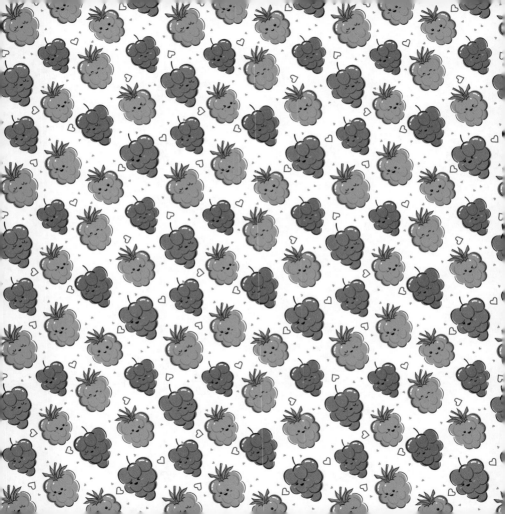

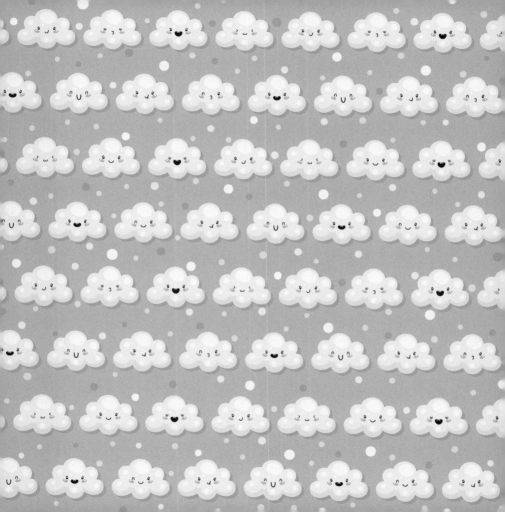

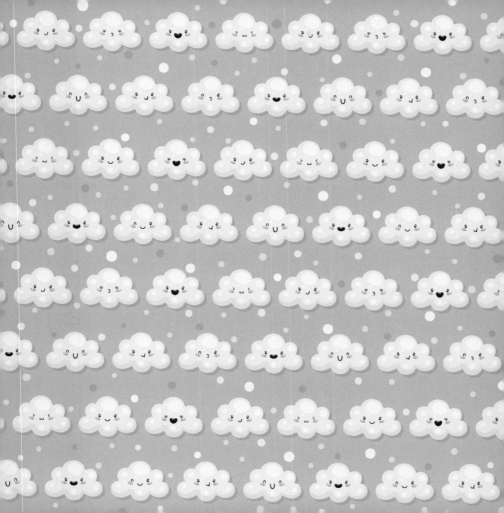

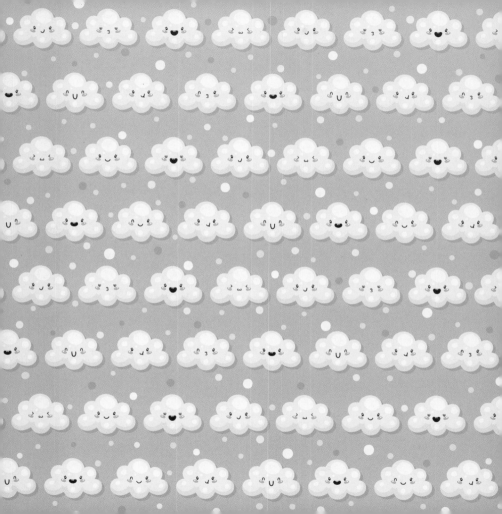

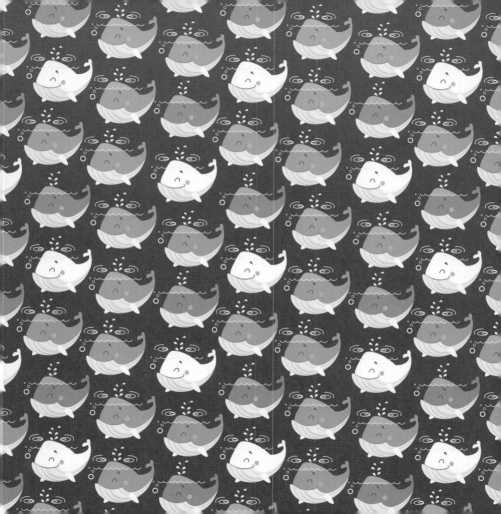

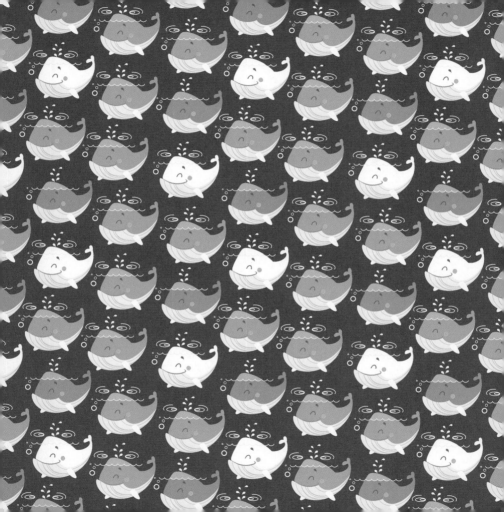

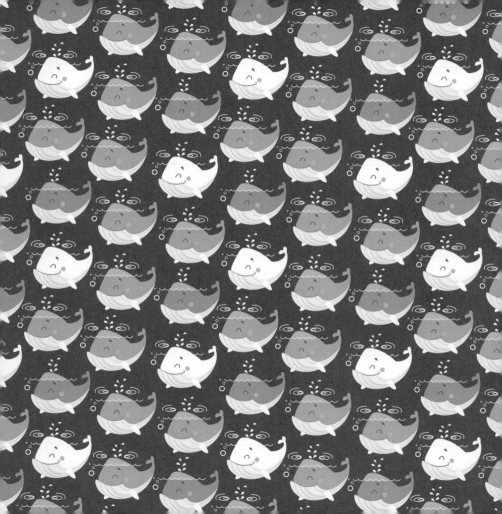

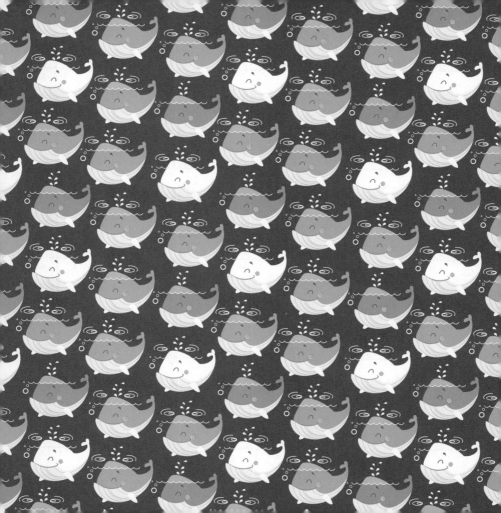

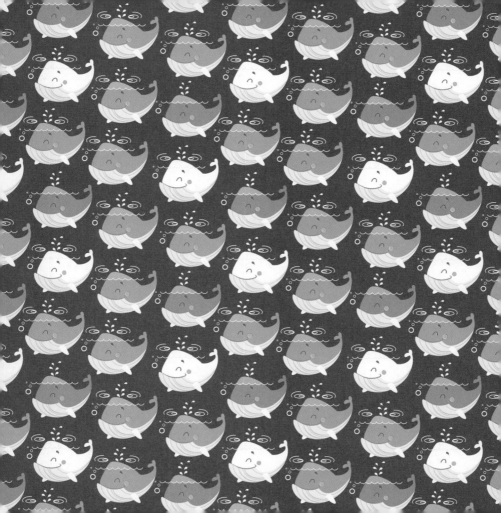

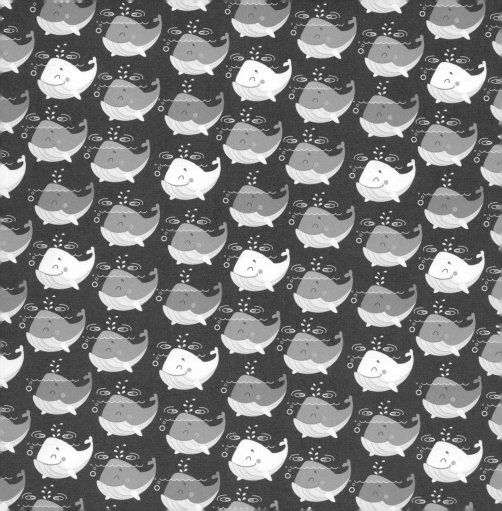

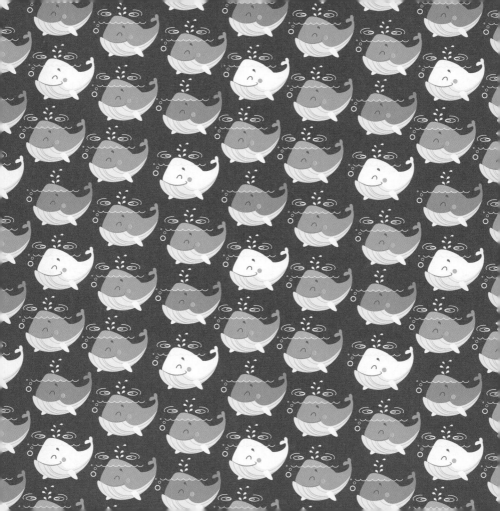

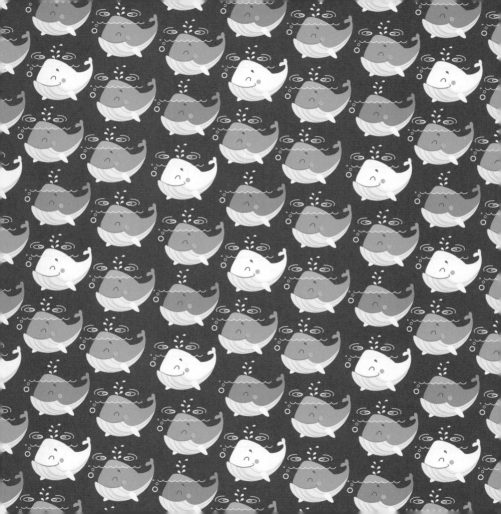

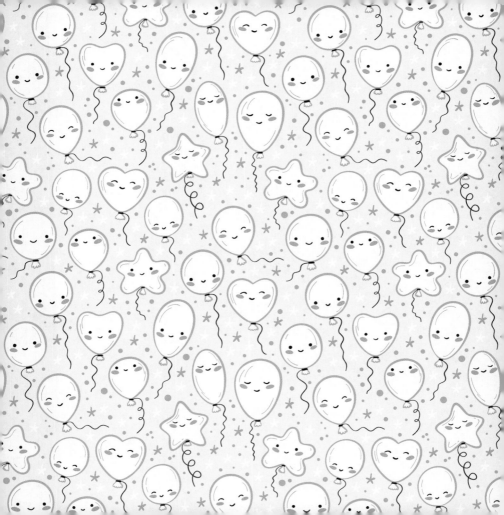

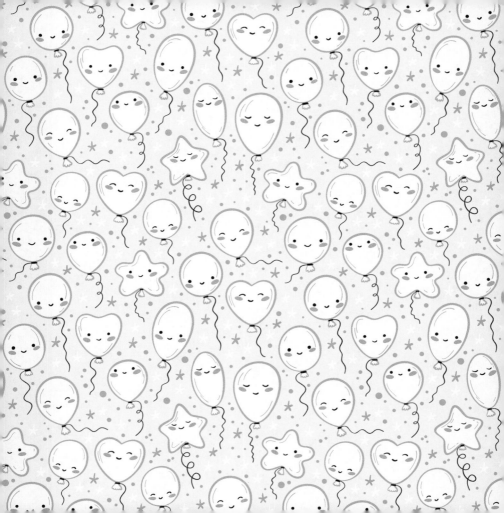

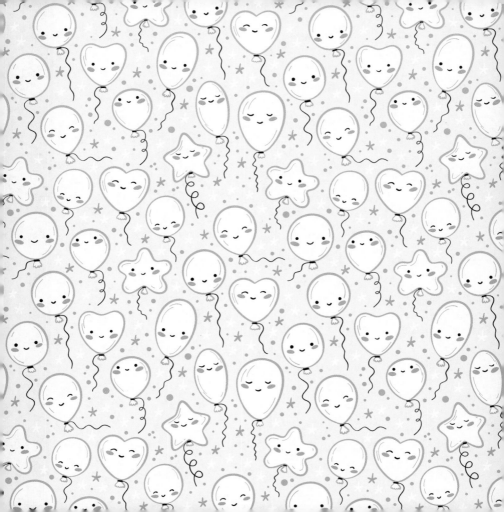

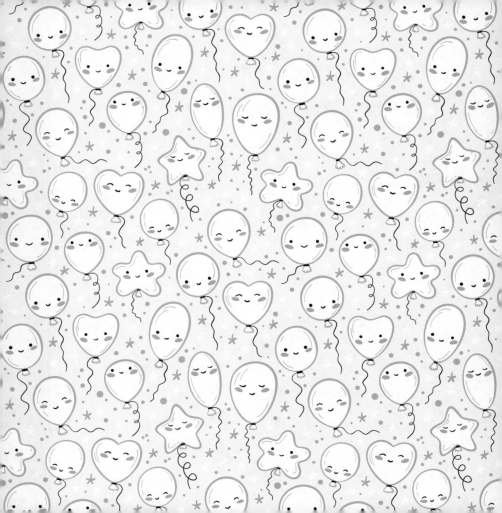

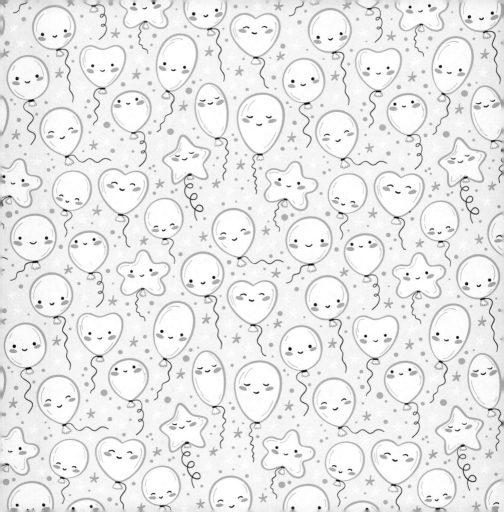

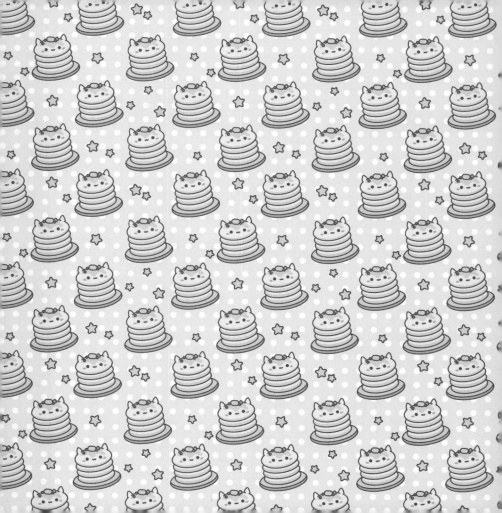

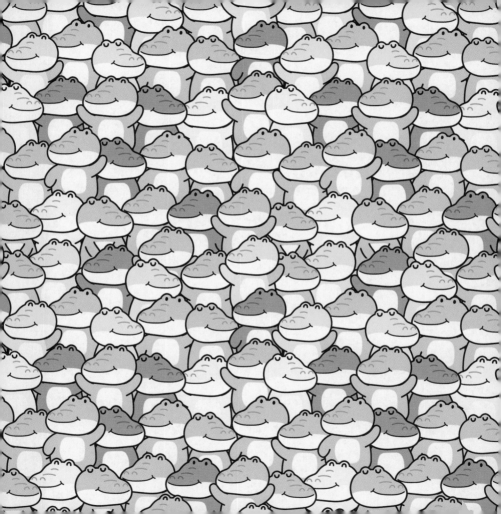

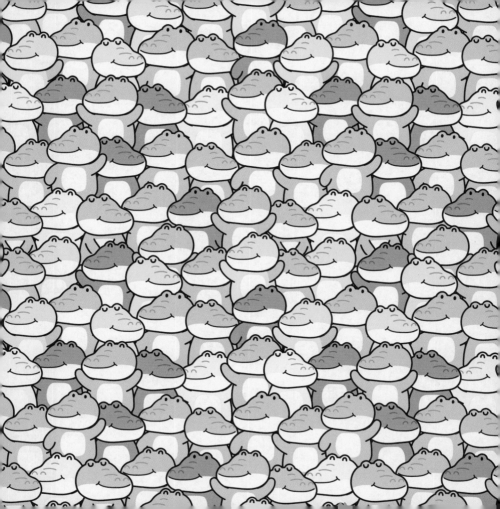

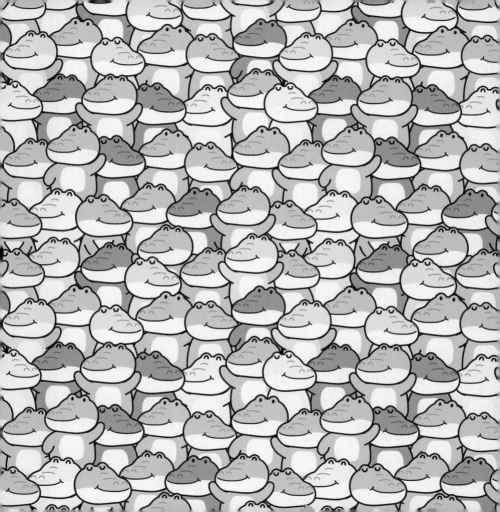

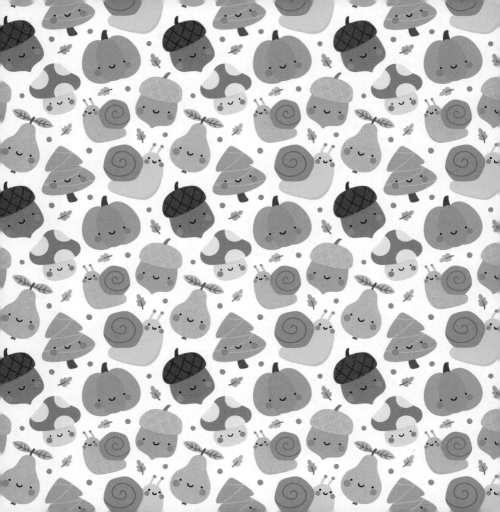

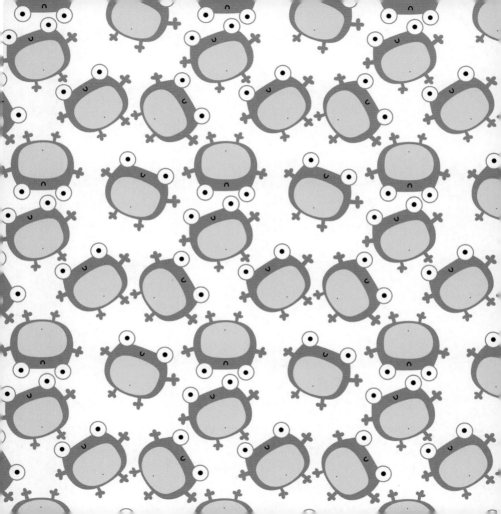

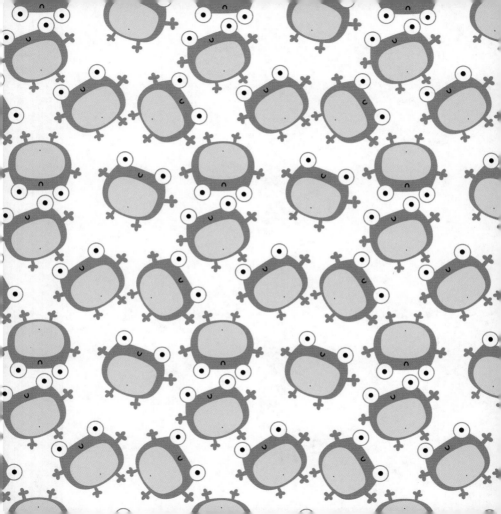

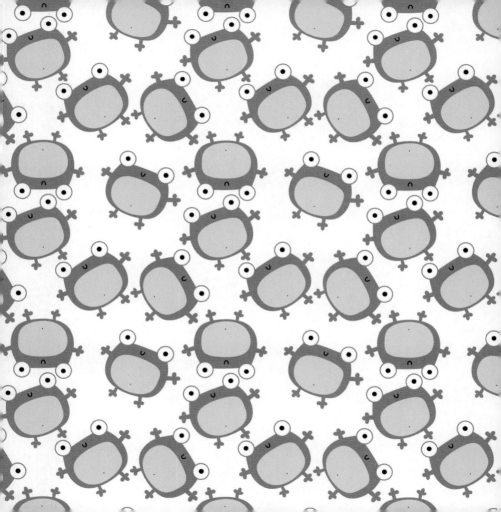

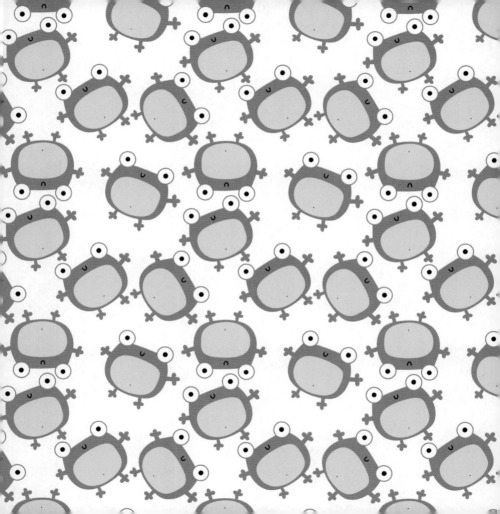

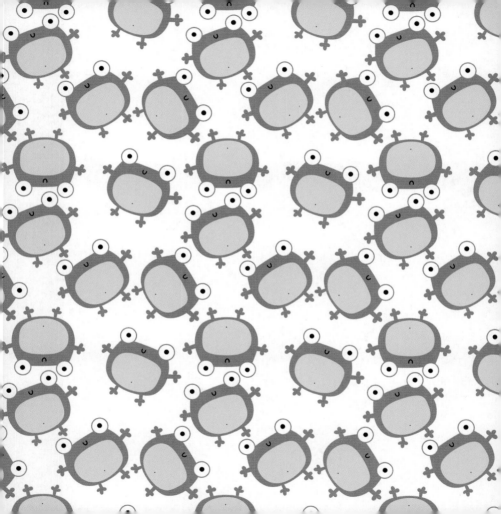

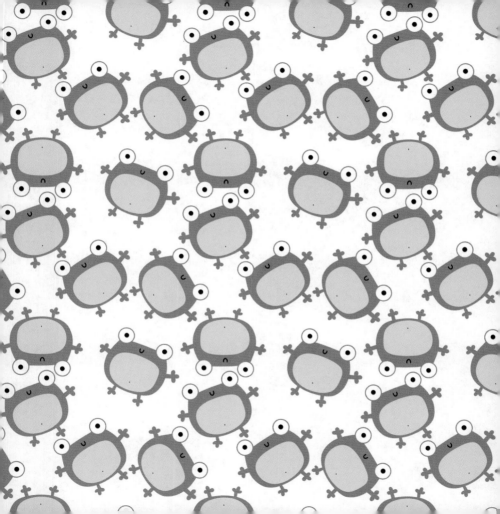

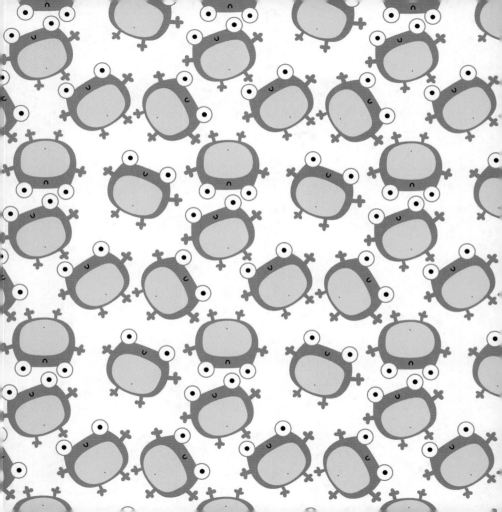

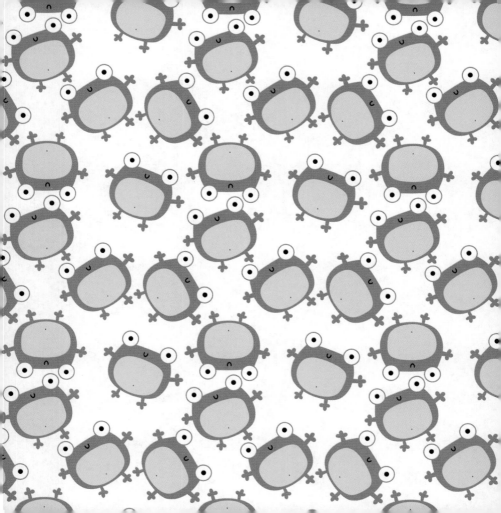

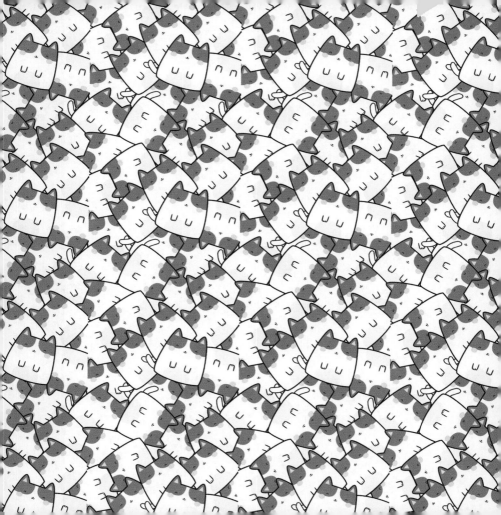

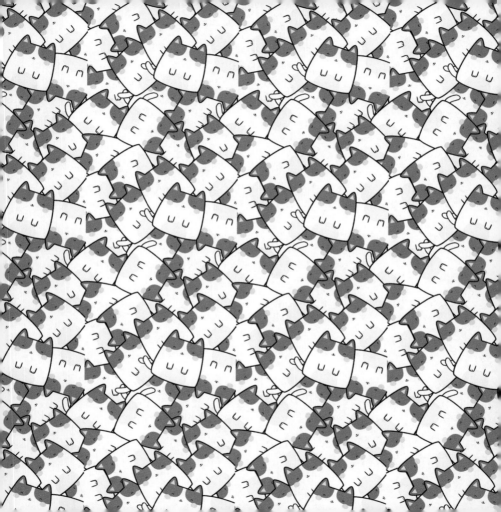

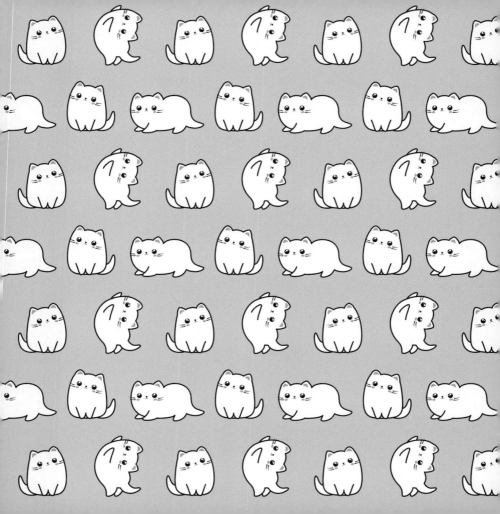

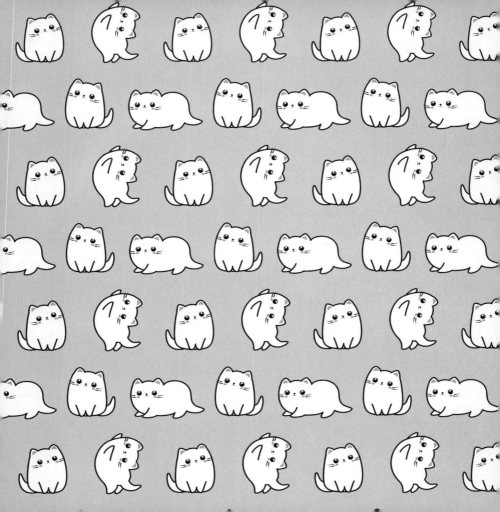

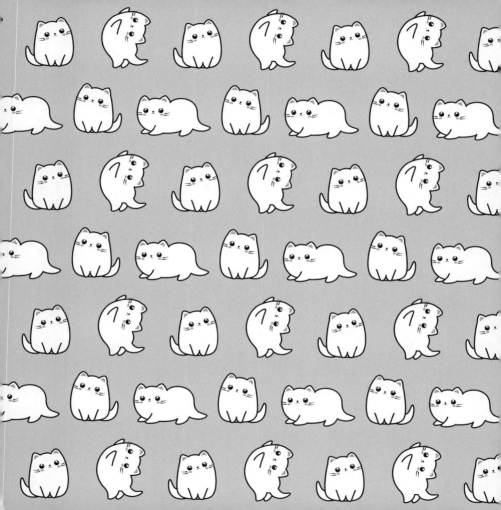

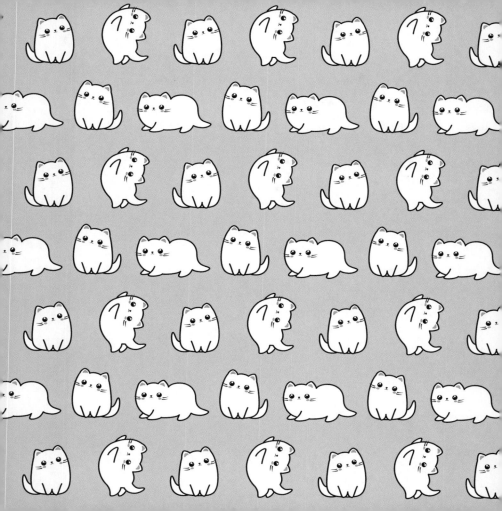

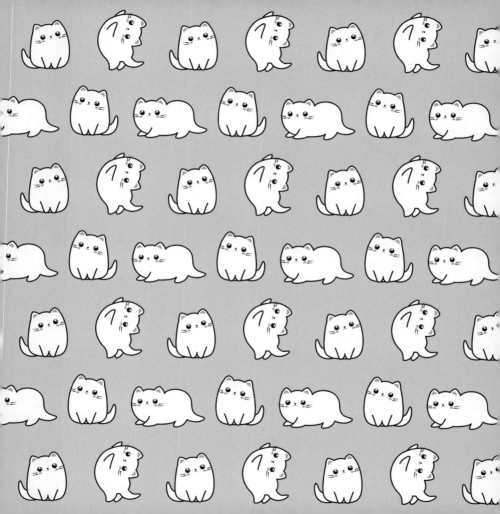

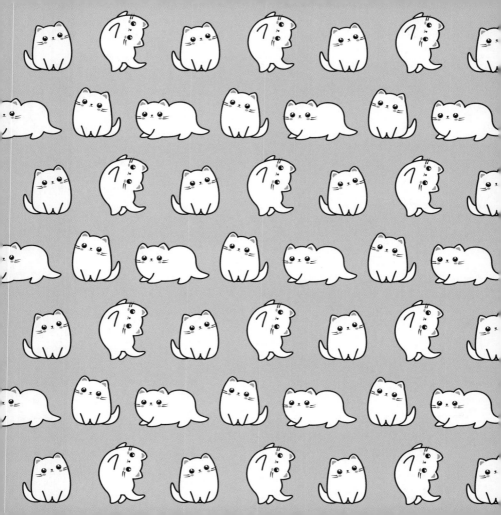

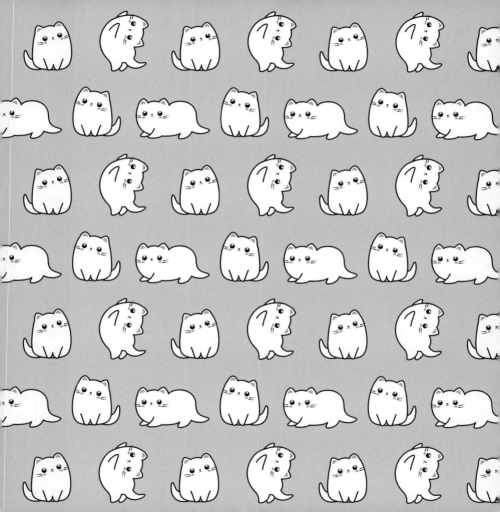

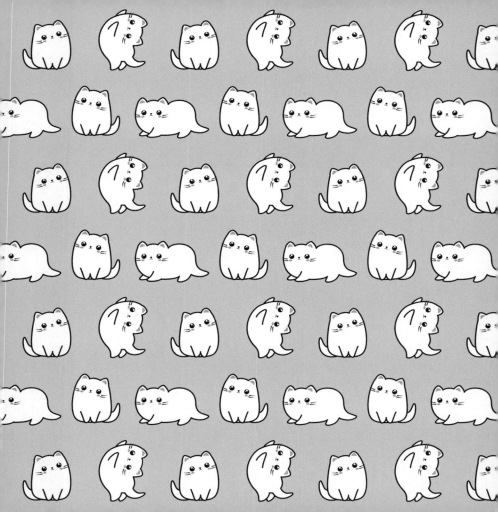